I0617960

Travis I. Sivart

27 Thoughts
on
Profound Sayings

Travis I. Sivart

Travis I. Sivart

27 Thoughts on Profound Sayings
27 Thoughts on Life Series, Book 4

Copyright © 2019 Travis I. Sivart

Cover Design by Travis I. Sivart
Edited by Tara Moeller

All rights reserved.

ISBN: 978-1-954214-46-0

Talk of the Tavern Publishing Group

Travis I. Sivart

Enjoying what you're reading?
Want a free eBook?

Go to TravisISivart.com/FreeBook

Travis I. Sivart

Dedication

This book is dedicated to all those great folks who I met at countless events, conventions, parties, online, and so many other places, that love words as much as I do.

Travis I. Sivart

Contents

Travis I. Sivart

Introduction

I grew up with people quoting wise sayings from bygone eras, or maybe it was just stuff the crazy old man at the gas station would say. When I was very young, many of these didn't make much sense, and by the time I got older I had heard them so many times that I never even thought about the meanings. Until I grew up and had heard these phrases countless times in many variations, only then did I realize these were staples of wisdom.

I have decided to take what I consider the most important of these and explain them, because what we see and hear too often become assimilated into our environment and we no longer see them as special and interesting.

I think these pearls of wisdom should be cherished, and I hope that this book makes you also cherish the value of these one-line sayings.

Travis I. Sivart

1. Those Who Fit In, Rarely Stand Out

You have a couple of choices in life on how to present yourself. The first is to conform and fit in. It is a safe choice, with little judgement and often allows you to be fully accepted by those around you. The second is to be more than what everyone else is - this doesn't mean rebelling for the sake of being different, it is so much more than that – and be yourself in the truest form.

Standing out means you show your unique nature, ideas, talents, differences, or whatever. People who do this are the movers and shakers, the trendsetters, and perhaps most importantly, the ones that change the world in large and small ways.

Standing out takes extreme courage and a lot of emotional and mental stamina. It helps to have the ability to not care what others think, but still be able to look at yourself with a critical eye (otherwise you may just be an attention-seeking, self-centered jerk). But if you can do this right, you can do more than change the world – you can change a single person's whole reality by being a positive influence.

Travis I. Sivart

2. Be True to Yourself

So many of us, myself included at times, have tried to please everyone around us. And I speak from experience when I say that no one ends up happy from that sort of behavior. You might be able to do it for a short time, but in the long run, it is a recipe for disaster.

Being true to yourself is not about being selfish, greedy, or taking from anyone else. Instead, it is about making yourself happy and successful in your endeavors in life, and also being honest with yourself about yourself. If you can be happy - truly happy - with yourself and who you are and what you are doing, then others will be attracted to you and gravitate to you.

Petty people will talk about you, put you down, and judge you. And that's ok, it is just who they are, and they are more concerned with you than themselves – thus, not being true to themselves. You do your thing, and life will present opportunities and you will be so much happier.

Travis I. Sivart

3. Many a Slip Between the Cup & the Lip

Variations: Shit Happens.

When you are on the road to success you will not make it in the first few steps, or often even in the first hundred steps. The point of this saying is to let you know that it is ok to have setbacks, screw-ups, failures, and so on. The point is that eventually you will get where you're going, and accomplish what it is that you set out to do, so don't give up. Giving up is for losers, trying again is for winners.

Travis I. Sivart

4. Know Thyself

The hardest thing is being introspective and knowing your own hopes, fears, wants, desires, and goals. It takes a lot of damn work! But, take it from me, it is so worth it. And the hard work that follows to do what it is you want to do, to get where you want to go, and accomplish the incredible things you want to do, is so worth it.

Dig deep, explore your light side, dark side, and wishy-washy middle. Learn your own strengths and weaknesses, and admit to them. There is nothing wrong with it; in fact, it will only make you the better and stronger person once you know these things about yourself.

Travis I. Sivart

5. The Show Must Go On

Variations: Never Give Up, Never Surrender! One Step at a Time. No Quarter, No Mercy.

An old showbiz adage, but it applies to so many things other than stage or film. I recall Dory in *Finding Nemo* saying, "Just keep swimming!" and it means the same thing. Don't stop, just keep trying.

You cannot fail until you stop trying. So, to never fail all you have to do is try again. Also, no matter the setback, push forward until you achieve your goal. Nothing else in life can be more true. Of course, some folks might quote the phrase, "Know when to give up", but that is another entry that isn't in this book, and for pessimists. Unless your stalking someone who isn't interested, then just stop that crap.

Travis I. Sivart

6. Walk a Mile in Another's Shoes

Life is unique for each and every one of us – including you – just like everyone else! You cannot ever totally know what someone else is going through, unless you have gone through the exact same thing.

This is all about empathy, which is the ability to relate to someone. The drama-prone will argue that someone can never know the depths that they endure, but I assure you that they are just seeking attention. But you do need some basis of comparison before you can understand someone's problems.

Never assume that you really relate, let the other person bear their burden, but do know that you may sympathize without having experienced something specific.

Travis I. Sivart

7. The Journey of a Thousand Miles Begins With One Step

You cannot finish something until you begin it. It really is that simple. No matter what you want to accomplish, you cannot do that until you start down the path that leads to it, for good or ill. I encourage the good reasons, as opposed to the bad ones; such as drug addiction.

If you ever want to do something, just do it (to quote a famous advertising campaign) and move forward in your plans. Without starting, there is no success.

Travis I. Sivart

8. Don't Cry Over Spilled Milk

You sometimes fail. It's that simple. Don't spend too much time lamenting that point, just move on and forward. If you use all your energy boo-hooing over not succeeding, then you won't have time to succeed.

See the previous mention of not giving up.

Travis I. Sivart

9. Lie, Steal, & Cheat

A great Irish toast, usually done at weddings, and it goes something like this:

"May you never steal, lie, or cheat. But if you must steal, then steal away my sorrows. And if you must lie, lie with me all the nights of my life. And if you must cheat, then please cheat death, because I couldn't live a day without you."

But it holds a lot of meaning. Be honest in life, and give yourself to those you love. It makes life worth it.

Travis I. Sivart

10. Nose to the Grindstone

Back to the grind is another way to look at it. Working hard is how you get things in life.

Now this particular phrase comes from hardworking blacksmiths who would use their rounded wheel of a grindstone, keeping it spinning using a foot petal like old sewing machines, and leaning over to watch the blade they were sharpening to keep the edge smooth and clean.

It teaches the lesson of watching what you're doing with an intensity that lends itself to perfection in your task. It also leads you to focusing on that task, and keeping at it until it's done.

A well-used phrase that many folks have forgotten to look for the value within it.

Travis I. Sivart

11. Take Time to Smell the Flowers

Life is made of moments. Many people are so busy waiting for the big moments, they forget to enjoy the small things in life.

Stopping to smell the flowers is a way to remind you that all the big things in life – the long journeys, big events, monumental moments – are made up of many, many smaller ones. And you need to appreciate those small things. Look for the beauty every day, smell the flowers and soak up the millions of things that so many miss because they're too busy waiting for the next big thing (or lamenting the passing of some past thing) to truly enjoy life.

Travis I. Sivart

12. A Bird In the Hand Is Worth Two In the Bush

Don't gamble what you have for a chance that you will probably miss. Appreciate what you have. If you have worked hard and made something (as in you caught one bird and are holding it), don't toss it aside for a long shot (such as two birds hiding in the bush a bit away from you).

In all likelihood, you will let go of what you have and not get the other thing that you thought would be bigger or better.

This doesn't mean that you shouldn't try for bigger and better things, it only means don't give up what you have for a maybe.

Travis I. Sivart

13. Youth Is Wasted On the Young

As we age, we realize how much we did, and how much we didn't do. It is not so much about wisdom of experience, but often more about having regrets of not taking the chances and opportunities we were presented with when we were younger and full of energy, hope... and perhaps not so bitter or realistic as we are at later ages in life.

For you young folks out there; try that thing, take that risk, talk to that person, go on that trip. Go and do all the things. You are more likely to regret not doing things than regretting what you did do.

Travis I. Sivart

14. Time Flies When Having Fun

When you are occupied, especially while having fun, your mind and body are busy doing without a chance to be concerned with the passing of time. So you often don't notice such things when you're doing something you love.

When you are idle, you notice the passage of time, seeking something meaningful in the emptiness of waiting. But when you're doing, time flies.

And as you get older, time has a lot more meaning than when you're younger.

Travis I. Sivart

15. All Who Wander Are Not Lost

There is a charm in meandering. Wandering is an activity, and a learning experience all of its own.

Sometimes you don't need a plan or a set direction. This is how you often discover new, and unexpected things, by just going where the wind blows you.

It is seeking something, but nothing more specific than a new experience. And once you get the hang of wandering, it can quickly become a great path to new and exciting adventures.

Travis I. Sivart

16. K.I.S.S. (Keep It Simple, Stupid)

Planning everything down to the last detail is often the recipe for failure. There is an old saying that came before this, "no battle plan ever survives the first encounter with the enemy," often attributed to Colin Powell, but also to Field Marshal Helmuth Carl Bernard von Moltke (what a name!).

Basically this all means, go ahead and plan, but don't be inflexible in what happens once things begin to move. Keeping things simple allows you (and the people involved) to make better and quicker judgement calls once things are in motion.

Travis I. Sivart

17. Eye On the Prize

Or keep your eye on the ball is another way of saying it. This just encourages you to remember why you're doing what you're doing. Don't get caught up in the minutia, and be ready to change how you're doing things so you can reach whatever your goal is.

Don't get sidetracked or distracted and let other things pull you away from the one thing that you are aiming to achieve.

18. A Spoonful of Sugar Helps the Medicine Go Down

"You attract more flies with honey, than vinegar" is another version of this saying. If you have something you don't want to do, then perhaps a little incentive can make this a bit less difficult to swallow when doing the task.

This goes for having others (like employees, children, etc.) do things for you also. Having a reward at the end of the task, or even just giving encouraging words or praise, can often help inspire that person to do something they would normally complain about.

Travis I. Sivart

19. The World Is Your Oyster

You could say, "I have the world on a string," or even, "grab the world by the balls," and they would work. These are all sayings that lets you know that you can get many things, but you have to go out and get them.

No one is going to do all the things and let you have the rewards from their hard work. Also, if you do it then you will appreciate the end result so much more than if someone does it for you. It will hold more value because you worked for it.

Go out and shuck your oyster to find your pearl, reel in that string to get what's on the other end, or grab your challenge and take control so you can reap that reward!

Travis I. Sivart

20. Keep Calm and Carry On

Panic never helps. Losing control doesn't ever help you get further along. Keeping calm, staying in control, and taking that next step is the best way to achieve whatever it is you want to do.

Carrying on is important also. Never giving up, one foot in front of the other, chin up, and all that. The surest way to fail is to stop trying.

Travis I. Sivart

21. Birds of a Feather, Flock Together

"Like attracts like," and "You are the people you surround yourself with," are all ways of saying that the people closest to you will influence you, your world, how you behave, and your level of success.

Many people encourage others to surround themselves with people they'd like to be like, or people smarter than themselves, or whatever. The point is that we assimilate habits, behaviors, and patterns from what we see around us. So make sure the people around you are the kind of person you want to be.

Travis I. Sivart

22. Two Wrongs Don't Make a Right

Someone yells at you, you yell back. Things escalate.

In a world where we live by "an eye for an eye, everyone ends up blind."

Treating others how they treat you when it is violent, negative, aggressive, harmful, or destructive only leads to bad things.

Don't do more wrong or harmful things and expect things to get better. Find a way that is truly better and helpful instead.

23. No Man Is an Island

Every individual is influenced by, and influences, people around them. Whether this is as simple as interacting (or not interacting) with people at a store, dealing with co-workers, or living with your family, we all have people that rely on us or that we rely on.

Our bosses pay us, our employees do work for us, the farmer raises crops and meats, the city workers build roads, and so on. No one person can be completely alone when in a society. We all affect, and in turn are affected by, others. No one can do it all by themselves.

Travis I. Sivart

24. There's No Such Thing as a Free Lunch

"Everything has a price," is another way of saying this. For everything you get in life, someone had to work for it. And if you got it, and you didn't work for it then someone else did, and you may now owe them in some fashion.

Things in life don't just fall from the sky into your lap. If you want something, then working for it is how to get it.

And if you are getting things without putting the work in, you may just be using others and not be a very nice person.

In a final thought, keep in mind that sometimes just appreciating what you get is payment enough.

Travis I. Sivart

25. There's No Place Like Home

When I speak of home, I mean the home that you make for yourself. The comfortable place that you go to so you can get away from the world for a little while. This might be your house or apartment, it might a group of friends, one special person, or any number of other places.

Home is where the heart is, is another saying, and these two go hand in hand. That one special place where you are just relaxed, calm, feel safe, and comforted is a special place... and there is no other place in the world like it.

This doesn't have to be a place with blood relatives, but it can be. This doesn't have to be the town you grew up in, but it can be. Or it could be with a group of strangers, hiking up a mountain, or some other adventure.

Your home is just for you, and there no other place in the world like it for you.

Travis I. Sivart

26. Beauty Is In the Eye of the Beholder

Many parents proudly post, or hold up, photos of their children. They beam and ask, "Aren't they beautiful?" and the rest of us often swallow nervously, nod awkwardly, and look for the nearest escape route. Or it might be your old beat-up car, or that dilapidated cabin on a lake that you went to every summer as a kid.

These things are beautiful because of the meaning and emotional value they hold for a person, rather than any particular physical feature or attribute.

In art, music, poetry, and other creative outlets beauty is very personal and individualistic. What one finds breathtaking, others may pass over with a shrug or an eye-roll. But again, it is that personal connection that goes deeper than the surface that you see that makes it beautiful.

So love what you love, and let others love what they love. And try to smile when they make you look at it with them.

Travis I. Sivart

27. You Can Lead a Horse to Water, but You Can't Make It Drink

This is most often used to refer to a person who you are trying to share wisdom or knowledge with. You can share what you know or have experienced, but you can't make them heed what you're telling them.

Some things people just have to learn on their own, and no amount of leading, talking, sharing, yelling, cajoling, or other forms of enticement will make them get what you mean.

Other people just refuse to listen to lessons from others, thinking they know better and wouldn't have to learn the hard way. Perhaps they are right, but they may also be wrong.

I'm pretty sure most of us have been led to water more than once, and refused to drink.

Travis I. Sivart

Enjoying what you're reading?
Want a free eBook?

Go to TravisISivart.com/FreeBook

About the Author

Travis I. Sivart lives in a state of constant flux between Richmond, VA and Washington, DC with his son and cats. He is not just an author but also father, public speaker, cook, pipe smoker, cat & squirrel lover, internet radio host, and so much more.

Travis I. Sivart is a Jack-Of-All-Trades. He has worked in mundane jobs such as restaurants, retail, construction, DMV, Notary, tech help, and more as well as more exotic trades such as; singing pirate, exorcist and paranormal researcher, Duke, cigar and pipe connoisseur, master of dungeons, a knight, therapist, minister, King, and has degrees in religion and metaphysics.

Travis I. Sivart writes steampunk, social DIY, science fiction, fantasy, young adult, speculative fiction, horror, and more.

You can find Travis at www.TravisISivart.com.

Travis I. Sivart

If you enjoyed this book...

Please let others know by reviewing it on Amazon or Goodreads, and let others know your thoughts!

Other books by Travis I. Sivart:

Aetheric Elements: The Rise of a Steampunk Reality

Automatons and airships, bustles and beasts, corsets and curses, dandies and dastardly deeds, all await you as you explore the cultures which evolved into a Steampunk industrial civilization. An anthology of nineteen tales of terror, mystery, and adventure.

Steampunk For Simpletons: A Fun Primer For Folks Who Aren't Sure What Steampunk Is All About

A primer followed by a guided tour through the world of steampunk, from the basics such as where to go and what to do, to the aesthetic of the arts within steampunk.

Journal of a Stranger

The thoughts, ideas, philosophies, and inspirations of a time traveling adventurer. Delving into the psychology of man, life's eternal questions, burning passions, and the quirky pseudo-science of his mind, and more.

The Downfall: Harbinger

The Talisman came again, but this time it didn't leave. The magical emanations of the comet have brought terrors from the bowels of the earth and increased the powers of an insane necromancer. The chaos above brought out others seeking to wrest control of the land. Five people from different walks of life are thrown together by these events with the knowledge that the world as they know it is ending.

Travis I. Sivart